COWS
ON THE FARM

Susan Markowitz Meredith

ROURKE PUBLISHING
www.rourkepublishing.com

www.rourkepublishing.com

PHOTO CREDITS: Title Page: © Dariusz Gora; Page 3: © Jeanne Hatch; Page 5: © Chris_Elwell; Page 7: © Paulo Carvalno; Page 8: © Dan70; Page 9: Jasmin Merdan, © VLIET, © GlobalP, © fotogaby; Page 11: © GlobalP; Page 12: © Jodi Jacobson; Page 13: © gregul; Page 15: © Hedda Gjerpen; Page 17: © ElementalImaging; Page 19: © lucato, © andymagic; Page 20: © VLIET, © steverts; Page 21: © 2windspa, © genekrebs, © eeandrey; Background: © FuzzMartin; Page 22: © Julián Rovagnati

Edited by Precious McKenzie

Cover by Nicola Stratford, Blue Door Publishing
Interior design by Renee Brady

Library of Congress Cataloging-in-Publication Data

Meredith, Susan, 1951-
Cows on the farm / Susan Markowitz Meredith.
   p. cm. -- (Farm animals)
Includes bibliographical references and index.
ISBN 978-1-61590-265-1 (alk. paper)
ISBN 978-1-61590-505-8 (soft cover)
1. Cows--Juvenile literature. 2. Farm life--Juvenile literature. 3. Ranches--Juvenile literature. I. Title.
SF197.5.M47 2011
636.2--dc22

                          2010009851

Rourke Publishing
Printed in the United States of America, North Mankato, Minnesota
033010
033010LP

www.rourkepublishing.com - rourke@rourkepublishing.com
Post Office Box 643328 Vero Beach, Florida 32964

Table of Contents

Cows Everywhere   4

Cows Close Up   10

Farm Life   16

Glossary   23

Index   24

Cows Everywhere

Cows are important farm animals. Many farmers around the world raise cows, or female **cattle**, for their milk.

FUN FACT

Some farmers today raise cattle for their meat, or beef. There are many breeds of beef cattle.

Cattle often live together in a large group called a herd.

For thousands of years, people have raised cattle. At first, people used the animals for their meat and hides, and for pulling heavy loads.

Modern cattle were once wild oxen. These ancient oxen roamed all over Europe, Asia, and north Africa.

Early farmers liked the milk from some cows better than others. Using **breeding**, farmers formed large groups of **dairy** cattle whose cows gave high-quality milk.

Popular Breeds of Dairy Cattle

Holstein-Friesian cows produce more milk than other breeds.

Jersey cows produce less milk than other breeds, but their milk tastes very rich.

Guernsey cows produce rich-tasting milk.

Brown Swiss cows come from Switzerland. Their milk is ideal for making cheese.

Cows Close Up

Cows have large bodies. Their coats are white, black, reddish brown, or a combination of these colors. Most cows have short hair.

Every cow has an **udder**. This bag-like **organ** hangs from the cow's body and holds milk. Dairy cows have large udders.

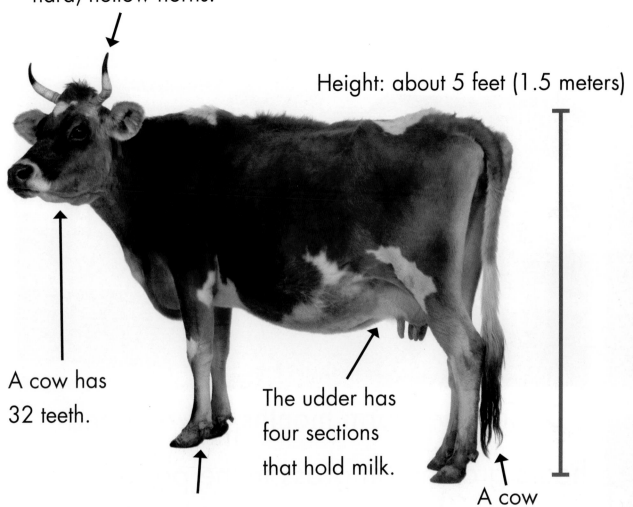

Some cows have hard, hollow horns.

Height: about 5 feet (1.5 meters)

A cow has 32 teeth.

The udder has four sections that hold milk.

A cow's hooves are divided.

A cow swishes her tail to shoo away insects.

During the warm months, cows spend hours grazing on grass in the pasture. Farmers also feed cattle chopped constalks, barley, cottonseed, or hay.

Every day, a cow eats up to 80 pounds (36kg) of food and drinks 30-40 gallons (114-151 liters) of water.

The food that cows eat is hard to **digest**. So they chew it at two different times.

At first, a cow chews her food just to get it wet. Then she swallows it. Later she brings the same food, called cud, up from her stomach to chew again.

FUN FACT
All cattle have four-part stomachs that digest food in the same way.

With no upper cutting teeth in front, cows tear off grass by moving their heads.

Farm Life

A cow cannot make milk until she gives birth to a calf. Most young cows, or **heifers**, have their first calf at age two.

After giving birth, a mother cow produces milk for about 10 months. To keep making milk, the cow must give birth to a new calf every year.

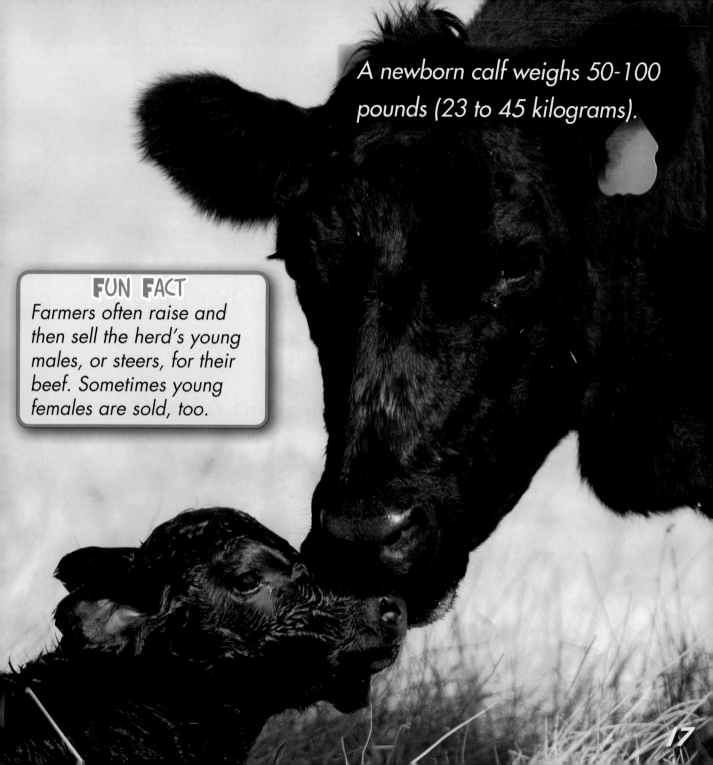

A newborn calf weighs 50-100 pounds (23 to 45 kilograms).

FUN FACT
Farmers often raise and then sell the herd's young males, or steers, for their beef. Sometimes young females are sold, too.

Cows need milking every day of the year. Many farmers milk their cows once in the early morning and once in the evening.

FUN FACT
Before milking begins, every worker washes off the cow's udder to remove dirt and germs.

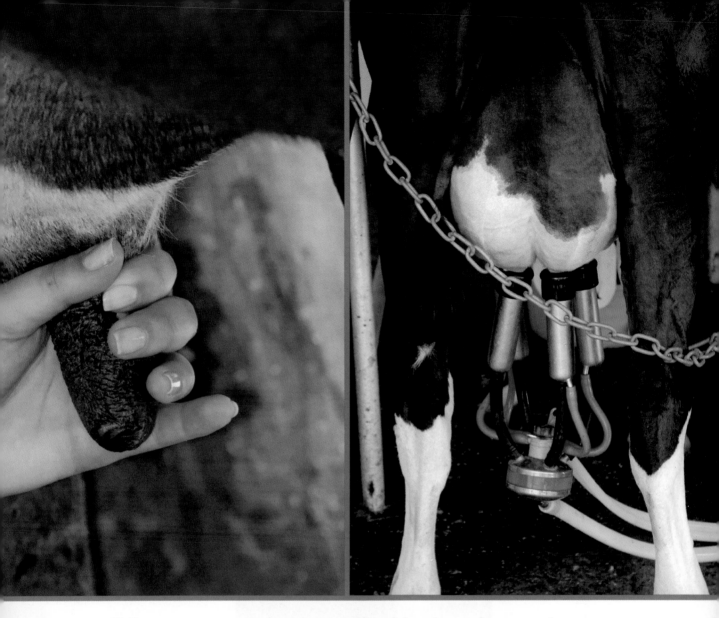

On small farms, cows may be milked by hand. Most large farms use special machines to milk the cows in a building called the milking parlor.

How Dairy Products Get to Your Table

Every day, a single cow produces 5 to 8 gallons (19-30 liters) of milk.

A large tank stores the cow milk and keeps it cool until a dairy truck picks it up.

A **refrigerated** truck carries the milk to a dairy factory.

Dairy factories, called **creameries**, use the milk to make butter, cheese, cottage cheese, yogurt, ice cream, whipped cream, and sour cream.

Creameries deliver dairy products to your local grocery store.

Hundreds of millions of cows live on Earth today. The milk of dairy cows nourishes people all over the world. People also rely on beef from cows.

Thank you, cows!

GLOSSARY

breeding (BREED-ing): a method for producing more animals with certain qualities, such as good-tasting milk

cattle (KAT-uhl): cows, bulls, and steers raised for their food or hides

creameries (KREEM-ur-ees): factories that make and sell dairy products

dairy (DAIR-ee): milk-related; a dairy cow is raised for her milk

digest (DYE-jest): to break down food in certain organs so that the body can use it

heifers (HEF-urz): young cows that have not yet given birth to a calf

organ (OR-guhn): a body part that does a certain job

refrigerated (ri-FRIJ-uh-ray-tud): something very cold on the inside that often stores food or drink

udder (UHD-ur): the baglike organ of a female cow, sheep, or goat that produces milk

Index

beef   4, 17, 22

breeds   9

calf   16, 17

cattle   4, 5, 6, 7, 12, 14

cud   14

farm(s)   4, 19

farmers   4, 8, 12, 17, 18

food   13, 14

grazing   12

milk   4, 8, 9, 10, 11, 16, 18, 19, 20, 21, 22

milking   18, 19

oxen   7

stomach(s)   14

Websites to Visit

www.kreiderfarms.com/index.php?id=565

www.cyberspaceag.com/farmanimals/default.htm

www.ansi.okstate.edu/breeds/cattle/

www.nichd.nih.gov/milk/kids/kidsteens.cfm

www.kidsfarm.com/

About the Author

Susan Markowitz Meredith enjoys learning new things about animals, including those on the farm. She especially likes to share what she discovers with young readers. Besides writing books, Ms. Meredith has also produced TV shows for young thinkers.